HANDLE
WITH CARE

Emotions, Finance, Sexuality

PARTICIPANT'S GUIDE

FOCUS
THE FAMILY

TYNDALE HOUSE PUBLISHERS, INC.
Carol Stream, Illinois

Essentials of Marriage: Handle with Care
Participant's Guide

Focus on the Family and the accompanying logo and design are federally registered trademarks of Focus on the Family, Colorado Springs, CO 80995.

A Focus on the Family book published by Tyndale House Publishers, Carol Stream, Illinois 60188

TYNDALE is a registered trademark of Tyndale House Publishers, Inc. Tyndale's quill logo is a trademark of Tyndale House Publishers, Inc.

All Scripture quotations, unless otherwise indicated, are taken from the *Holy Bible, New International Version*®. NIV®. Copyright © 1973, 1978, 1984 by International Bible Society. Used by permission of Zondervan Publishing House. All rights reserved.

Cover design by Jessie McGrath

Cover image (top) copyright © by Tarek El Sombati/iStockphoto. All rights reserved.

Cover photo of bride and groom copyright © by Image Source Photography/Veer. All rights reserved.

Cover photo of couple holding boxes copyright © by George Doyle/Getty Images. All rights reserved.

Cover photo of couple near fire copyright © by Corbis Photography/Veer. All rights reserved.

ISBN: 978-1-58997-561-3

Printed in the United States of America
1 2 3 4 5 6 7 / 15 14 13 12 11 10 09

CONTENTS

QUICK START GUIDE FOR COUPLES

Whether you're studying in a group, as a couple, or individually, this book is for you. It's packed with discussion questions, advice, biblical input, and application activities.

But maybe all you'd like to do right now is watch the accompanying DVD and talk about it with your spouse. If so, go directly to the "Catching the Vision" section of each chapter. There you'll find the discussion questions you're looking for.

When you have more time, we encourage you to explore the other features in this book. We think you'll find them . . . essential!

For even more help with your relationship, go to
focusonthefamily.com/marriage.

WELCOME!

If there's anything you don't need, it's one more thing to do.

Unless, of course, that one thing might make the *other* things a whole lot easier.

We can't guarantee that this course will take all the challenge out of your marriage. It won't keep you from forgetting your anniversary, thaw all the icy silences, or make your spouse alphabetize the shoes in your closet.

But it *will* help you understand why you're married, how to stay that way, and how to enjoy it to the fullest. That's because you'll learn the essentials—what's vital to a healthy relationship, keys to working out your differences, and what God considers most important in "holy matrimony."

In other words, you'll discover how to be the husband or wife you really want to be.

That takes effort, but it doesn't take boredom or busy work. So we've designed this course to be provocative and practical. At its heart is an entertaining, down-to-earth video series featuring many of today's most popular marriage experts. And in your hands is the book that's going to make it all personal for you—the Participant's Guide.

In each chapter of this book, you'll find the following sections:

Finding Yourself. Take this survey to figure out where you stand on the subject at hand.

Catching the Vision. Use this section as you watch and think about the DVD.

Digging Deeper. This Bible study includes Scripture passages and thought-provoking questions.

Making It Work. Practice makes perfect, so here's your chance to begin applying principles from the DVD to your own marriage.

Bringing It Home. To wrap up, a licensed counselor affiliated with Focus on the Family offers encouraging advice you can use this week.

Whether you're using this book as part of a group or on your own, taking a few minutes to read and complete each chapter will bring the messages of the DVD home.

And isn't that exactly where you and your spouse need it most?

Note: Many issues addressed in this series are difficult ones. Some couples may need to address them in greater detail and depth. The DVD presentations and this guide are intended as general advice only, and not to replace clinical counseling, medical treatment, legal counsel, or financial guidance.

Focus on the Family maintains a referral network of Christian counselors. For information, call 1-800-A-FAMILY and ask for the counseling department. You can also download free, printable brochures offering help for couples at http://www.focusonthefamily.com/marriage/articles/brochures.aspx.

Chapter 1

ONE STEP AT A TIME

When you got engaged, you probably thought you were marrying the person of your dreams. After the wedding day, though, you realized your spouse had some annoying habits.

Suddenly the person who could do no wrong was in need of a makeover.

Maybe you started a reforming program, only to discover that you don't have enough resources or power to change your spouse. Now your refrain sounds something like this:

"Cathy is always late for everything. Last week I decided to go on to church without her, and then for some reason she gets mad at me!"

"Bob thinks it's funny to start burping contests at the table with our boys. It is *very* embarrassing."

Chances are that you married your spouse not just because you had similarities, but also for the differences. You may have been attracted to these differences because of your need to feel completed by another person. These traits may be endearing before marriage, but can disrupt the relationship afterward.

Do you have to live with these habits? Should loving this person be enough to enable you to overlook them? And if you can't, should you feel guilty?

—Sheryl DeWitt
Licensed Marriage and Family Therapist[1]

Identifying Your Needs

Here's a questionnaire to get you thinking about how you relate to the subject of improving your marriage.

1. Before you were married, which of the following did you agree with? Which do you agree with now?
   ____ "You can't change your spouse."
   ____ "Once we're married, he [or she] will change."
   ____ "I'll get used to him [or her]."
   ____ "I wouldn't change a thing."
   ____ "If things don't change, I'll go crazy."

2. When it comes to changing your spouse's behavior, which of the following have you tried? What were the results?
   ____ nagging
   ____ prayer
   ____ an extreme makeover
   ____ counseling
   ____ brain surgery
   ____ recommending a book
   ____ setting a good example
   ____ bribery
   ____ other _____

3. Let's say your spouse has a habit of leaving dirty clothes on the floor. Which of the following describes your most likely response?
   ____ resentful silence
   ____ yelling, "Why don't you stop leaving dirty clothes on the floor?"

_____ picking up the clothes and being thankful that he or she isn't dead or having an affair

_____ starting small by asking him or her to pick up just the socks

_____ declaring a zero tolerance policy on all dirty laundry

_____ other _____

4. Would you rather lose one pound a week for six months, or a pound a day for a month? Why? _____

_____

5. Would you rather try to quadruple your savings account in 40 days or 40 years? Why? _____

_____

6. What might the two previous questions have to do with the process of improving your marriage? _____

CATCHING THE VISION

Watching and Discussing the DVD

In this DVD segment, Drs. John Trent and Greg Smalley present a little idea that gets big results: improving your marriage a step at a time instead of trying to leap the Grand Canyon in a single bound.

Small changes are doable—and they work. In fact, it's the little things that often make the difference between couples who do well and those who struggle. Making minor, frequent course corrections on your marital journey prevents panicky, wrenching attempts at change later. And when it comes to changing your spouse, keep your expectations small, too.

After viewing the DVD, use questions like these to help you think through what you saw and heard.

1. Do small changes or big ones work best when you're trying to do the following? Why?
   • turn up the volume on a car radio
   • color your hair
   • add salt to soup
   • be more honest with your spouse

2. How was Dr. John Trent's near-accident like some people's approach to married life? How might one or both spouses be "asleep at the wheel"? What kinds of things wake them up?

3. In each of the following cases, what small course corrections might help? What overcorrections might be too much?
   • You want your spouse to help more with household chores.
   • Your spouse thinks you spend too much time with your parents.
   • You read in a book that husbands and wives should pray together daily, and you've never done it once.
   • Your spouse says he or she would like "more physical affection."

4. How did John Trent solve his "pointing problem"? Would you use his pay-a-fine strategy in the following situations? If not, why not? If so, what would the fine be?
   • You keep forgetting to empty the cat litter box, leaving your spouse to take care of it.
   • Your spouse wants you to talk more.
   • Your spouse wants you to talk less.
   • You're usually late getting ready when you're supposed to go out for the evening.

5. Why did John Trent and his wife pay a babysitter and go to the food court once a week? Would that be a 2-degree change for you, a 45-degree change, or a 180-degree change? What might make a change like that worth it?

6. How is trying to get your spouse to change like pushing a rope? Which of the following do you think John Trent means when he suggests walking in the right direction while holding on to the rope?
    - being a good example to your spouse and encouraging any progress
    - telling your spouse where to go and controlling him or her
    - staying in step together and keeping your spouse close
    - other _____

7. Have you ever tried to make a change that was "too big"? If so, what happened? Why might one small change lead to another?

8. How would you answer someone who says, "My marriage needs big changes, not small ones"?

Bible Study

> A champion named Goliath, who was from Gath, came out of the Philistine camp. He was over nine feet tall. . . .
>
> David said to Saul, "Let no one lose heart on account of this Philistine; your servant will go and fight him."
>
> Saul replied, "You are not able to go out against this Philistine and

*fight him; you are only a boy, and he has been a fighting man from his
youth."*

*But David said to Saul . . . "The LORD who delivered me from the
paw of the lion and the paw of the bear will deliver me from the hand of
this Philistine."*

Saul said to David, "Go, and the LORD be with you."

*Then Saul dressed David in his own tunic. He put a coat of armor
on him and a bronze helmet on his head. David fastened on his sword
over the tunic and tried walking around, because he was not used to
them.*

*"I cannot go in these," he said to Saul, "because I am not used to
them." So he took them off. Then he took his staff in his hand, chose five
smooth stones from the stream, put them in the pouch of his shepherd's
bag and, with his sling in his hand, approached the Philistine. . . .*

*As the Philistine moved closer to attack him, David ran quickly to-
ward the battle line to meet him. Reaching into his bag and taking out
a stone, he slung it and struck the Philistine on the forehead. The stone
sank into his forehead, and he fell facedown on the ground.*

*So David triumphed over the Philistine with a sling and a stone;
without a sword in his hand he struck down the Philistine and killed
him. (1 Samuel 17:4, 32-34, 37-40, 48-50)*

1. How did small things make a big difference in this story?

2. What did Saul assume about the best way to change the situation?
   How might that attitude lead to discouragement?

3. What was the real reason for David's success?

4. How could this story serve as a pattern for changing things in a
   marriage?

When Jesus landed and saw a large crowd, he had compassion on them, because they were like sheep without a shepherd. So he began teaching them many things.

By this time it was late in the day, so his disciples came to him. "This is a remote place," they said, "and it's already very late. Send the people away so they can go to the surrounding countryside and villages and buy themselves something to eat."

But he answered, "You give them something to eat."

They said to him, "That would take eight months of a man's wages! Are we to go and spend that much on bread and give it to them to eat?"

"How many loaves do you have?" he asked. "Go and see."

When they found out, they said, "Five—and two fish."

Then Jesus directed them to have all the people sit down in groups on the green grass. So they sat down in groups of hundreds and fifties. Taking the five loaves and the two fish and looking up to heaven, he gave thanks and broke the loaves. Then he gave them to his disciples to set before the people. He also divided the two fish among them all. They all ate and were satisfied, and the disciples picked up twelve basketfuls of broken pieces of bread and fish. The number of the men who had eaten was five thousand. (Mark 6:34-44)

5. How did small things make a big difference in this story?

6. What did the disciples assume about the best way to change the situation?

7. What was the real reason why Jesus' approach worked?

8. How could this story serve as a pattern for changing things in a marriage?

He told them another parable: "The kingdom of heaven is like a mustard seed, which a man took and planted in his field. Though it is the smallest of all your seeds, yet when it grows, it is the largest of garden plants and becomes a tree, so that the birds of the air come and perch in its branches."

He told them still another parable: "The kingdom of heaven is like yeast that a woman took and mixed into a large amount of flour until it worked all through the dough." (Matthew 13:31-33)

9. Why do you suppose God seems to like using small things in big ways?

10. What's one small thing you think He's used to improve your marriage?

Applying the Principles

It's time to come up with your marital "flight plan" for this week. Here are three destinations; choose one. With your spouse if possible, pick from the corresponding list up to four "course corrections" that you're willing to make during the next six days. Write those corrections in the blanks next to the dots on your flight plan—in the order in which you'll make them.

To keep your plan specific, write an "estimated time of arrival" next to each course correction. For example, "Tuesday after dinner" might belong next to "Talk about feelings for five minutes." If the course correction is something you're pledging *not* to do (like "Avoid comparing my spouse to others, real or imagined"), write "as needed" next to it.

When you've determined your flight plan, ask God for help in carrying it out.

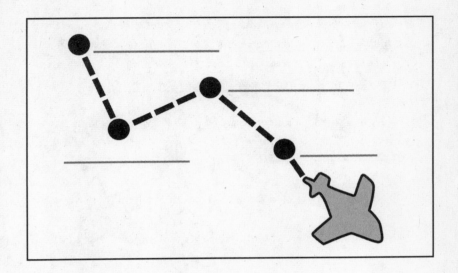

Destination: Better Communication

Possible course corrections:

- Make more eye contact during conversations.
- Find a quiet place to talk.
- Talk about feelings for five minutes.
- Go out to dinner and reminisce about our wedding.
- Send my spouse an e-mail or text message once a day.
- Don't use the phrases "You always" or "You never."
- Ask my spouse's opinion on a political issue and follow up with one or two clarifying questions.
- Share two personal prayer requests with my spouse.
- Ask my spouse to tell me when I'm talking too loudly or too softly.
- Avoid folding my arms, frowning, or looking distracted when we talk.

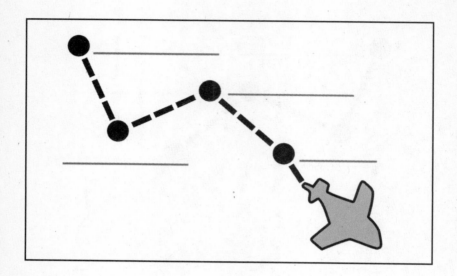

Destination: More Help from My Spouse with Household Chores

Possible course corrections:

- Thank my spouse for doing a chore in the past.
- Avoid criticizing my spouse for not doing a task in the way I would have done it.
- Ask my spouse to do a specific chore just once, at a specific time.
- Offer to do a task my spouse usually does.
- Avoid comparing my spouse to others, real or imagined.
- Reach agreement on which chores are necessary.
- Reach agreement on how often each chore needs to be performed.
- Offer to show my spouse how I perform a particular chore.
- Praise my spouse in front of another person for helping in the past.
- Reward my spouse for helping by taking him or her out for dessert.

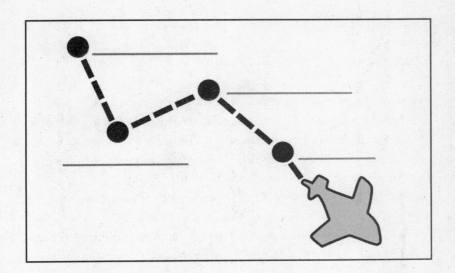

Destination: More Physical Affection Between Us

Possible course corrections:

- Hold hands while taking a walk or watching TV.
- Give or receive a back rub.
- Kiss before leaving for work.
- Hug when coming home from work.
- Tell my spouse about one of his or her most attractive physical features.
- Put on a different cologne or perfume each day.
- Go to bed an hour early one evening, and at the same time.
- Take a bath or shower together.
- Light scented candles in the bedroom.
- Talk about my spouse's favorite subject for at least 10 minutes.

Encouragement from a Counselor

Ask yourself why you want change. Is it for your own good only? Might the change make you feel better, but cause your mate to feel imprisoned? Or is the change to help eliminate behaviors that keep your spouse from growing emotionally and spiritually? In other words, are you helping to set your partner free or just restricting his or her freedom?

If changing the habit would truly benefit both of you, change may be worth trying. But keep these guidelines in mind:

1. *Address the problem honestly.* "Honey, it bothers me when you burp at the table. It teaches the children a bad habit, and it's rude and offensive to guests."

2. *Explain the benefit of change.* "Eating at the table will be more pleasant for all of us. The boys will also respect your table manners and you'll be a good testimony to our guests."

3. *Don't command change.* "You're such a slob at the table. Stop being so messy." Instead, *request* change. Your spouse will respond more favorably.

4. *Don't attack your mate.* "You are a horrible listener. It's no wonder no one talks to you." When you attack your spouse, you crush his or her spirit—and don't get much cooperation. Confront the problem; don't attack the person.

5. *Discuss ways to bring about change.* Change is hard. Let your spouse know that you're on his or her side. Help him or her find ways to change those habit patterns. If the problem is overeating, for instance, go with your spouse to the gym, cook healthy meals, and go out to eat less often. Be your mate's advocate.

6. *Encourage your spouse's growth.* "You're doing a great job. I'm really proud of the effort I see. Thank you for your dedication to making this change."

7. *Recognize that change takes time.* Be patient with your spouse. Praise little steps that you see. Everyone wants to feel successful. So don't discourage your mate with comments like, "This is taking forever. How many more times do we have to deal with this?" Discouragement stunts growth, but encouragement goes a long way in motivating change. Let your spouse know you're in this together for the long haul.

8. *Pray for your spouse.* God is ultimately the one who makes change possible in any of us. So pray for your mate's efforts. And since some behaviors may never change, ask God to give you grace to accept the differences between you and your spouse.

9. *Seek to change the habit, not the person.* It's possible to help your spouse drop an irritating habit—as long as it's the habit you're trying to change. If you're trying to alter your spouse's personality or temperament, you'll be fighting a losing battle that will end in frustration for both of you.

Take Susan and Lee, for example. Susan, an extremely social person, loves to stay after church to talk, is the last to leave a party, and likes to be the center of attention. In contrast, her husband Lee is reserved, prefers to be in the background, and is exhausted by socializing. Lee has learned to go to parties with Susan out of love for her. But she can't expect him to become a fan of social gatherings. She needs to appreciate his willingness to go with her and not try to make him the extrovert she is.

If you follow the aforementioned guidelines and don't meet with success, it's time to ask yourself whether the battle is worth it. Some habits are so engrained that if they don't involve moral issues or character flaws, it may be best to live with them. Bringing them up repeatedly may lead only to more bitterness and conflict.

Keep praying for your spouse. And when you think of him or her, focus on his or her positive traits—instead of that irritating habit.

—Sheryl DeWitt
Licensed Marriage and Family Therapist[2]

Chapter 2

GREAT SEX IN A GODLY MARRIAGE (PART 1)

Jill didn't know what to say when she opened Mark's gift. The pretty package had been a total surprise. "It just made me think of you," he'd told her.

Judging by the size of the box, she'd thought it might be a new scarf or a sampler of chocolates. The last thing she'd expected was this lace teddy.

Didn't Mark know she wasn't the lingerie type? She could imagine how big her thighs would look in this thing.

Sometimes she thought they'd never see eye to eye when it came to sex. They'd been married only a year, and already their differences were clear. What would things be like five years from now—if they made it that far?

—Rob Jackson
Licensed Professional Counselor[3]

Identifying Your Needs

What are your attitudes about the role of sex in marriage? Here's a survey to get you thinking about that.

1. Which of the following did you hear in some form when you were growing up? Do you think hearing that influenced you? Why or why not?

   ____ "Sex is only for married people."

   ____ "Sex is dirty."

   ____ "God created sex."

   ____ "Sex is only for reproduction."

   ____ "People lose interest in sex after they get married."

   ____ "Men want sex; women want love."

2. Which of the following do you think is the most important part of a good sexual relationship in marriage? Why?

   ____ good physical health

   ____ a sense of humor

   ____ trust

   ____ good personal hygiene

   ____ emotional closeness

   ____ physical attraction

   ____ spiritual commitment

   ____ other _____

3. Which of the following do you think most married couples struggle with?

   ____ how often to have sex

   ____ being too busy to have a love life

___ being too tired or stressed for sex
___ infidelity
___ pornography
___ lack of knowledge about sex
___ overcoming past sexual abuse

4. When was the last time you saw a marital sexual relationship portrayed positively on TV or in a movie? Do you see that often?

_____

5. Do you think Christians talk too much about the sexual part of marriage, not enough, or about the right amount? Why? _____

_____

6. Do you think most sex education classes do a good job of preparing people for marriage? Why or why not? _____

_____

CATCHING THE VISION

Watching and Discussing the DVD

"America's Family Coaches," Dr. Gary and Barb Rosberg, join forces with author Gary Thomas in this DVD segment to address a subject spouses need to talk about—but often don't.

Gary Thomas reveals that "chemistry" really does play a big part in God's plan for men and women. The Rosbergs share couples' answers to the question, "What do you need to have great sex in a godly marriage?"

After viewing the DVD, use questions like these to help you think through what you saw and heard.

1. Do you think most couples today know more about sex when they get married than couples 50 years ago did? If so, has it made marriages happier? Do you think today's brides and grooms understand the role of sex in marriage better than in the "olden days"? Why or why not?

2. Do you agree with Gary Thomas that God gave men a sex drive that renews their affection for their wives? Do you think it works as a "glue" in most marriages? Why or why not?

3. According to Gary Thomas, husbands are likely to feel closer to their wives after sex than they will after a long talk about feelings. If that's true, how could it affect the following aspects of a marriage?
   - the frequency of sexual relations
   - the husband's interest in conversation
   - the wife's interest in sex
   - the couple's overall sense of closeness

4. Which of the following would you expect a Puritan pastor to say? Why? Which of these statements best reflects the attitude toward sex that you learned growing up?
   - "Control yourself."
   - "Do not let your conjugal love grow lukewarm."
   - "Whatever feeleth good, doest thou it."
   - "An idle mind is the devil's playground."
   - other _____

5. Do you think the phrases "great sex" and "godly marriage" belong in the same sentence? Why or why not? Which of the following statements would you agree with? Why?
   - The more godly your marriage is, the greater the sex will be.
   - Truly godly people don't pursue great sex.
   - You can have great sex without being godly.
   - Godliness prevents great sex.

6. Research by Dr. Gary and Barb Rosberg revealed the following top "sex needs" among husbands. If you're a man, would you rank them in this order? If you had to add two others, what would they be? Why?
   - mutual satisfaction
   - connection
   - responsiveness
   - initiation
   - affirmation

7. The Rosbergs found the following love-life ingredients most valued among wives. If you're a woman, would you rank them in this order? If you had to add two others, what would they be? Why?
   - affirmation
   - connection
   - non-sexual touch
   - romance
   - spiritual intimacy

8. Why do you suppose "connection" and "affirmation" are the only two items on both lists? How might a husband and wife connect with each other despite their sexual differences? How might they affirm each other despite those differences?

Bible Study

Marriage should be honored by all, and the marriage bed kept pure, for God will judge the adulterer and all the sexually immoral. (Hebrews 13:4)

1. What are three ways in which you can "honor" marriage?

2. What does it mean for the marriage bed to be "pure"? What does this
    imply about how God views sex inside and outside of marriage?

[Lover]
I have come into my garden, my sister, my bride;
*   I have gathered my myrrh with my spice.*
*   I have eaten my honeycomb and my honey;*
*   I have drunk my wine and my milk.*
[Friends]
Eat, O friends, and drink;
*   drink your fill, O lovers.*
[Beloved]
I slept but my heart was awake.
*   Listen! My lover is knocking:*
*   "Open to me, my sister, my darling,*
*   my dove, my flawless one.*
*   My head is drenched with dew,*
*   my hair with the dampness of the night." . . .*
O daughters of Jerusalem, I charge you—
if you find my lover,
what will you tell him?
Tell him I am faint with love.
[Friends]
How is your beloved better than others,
*   most beautiful of women?*
*   How is your beloved better than others,*
*   that you charge us so?*
[Beloved]
My lover is radiant and ruddy,
*   outstanding among ten thousand.*

His head is purest gold;
his hair is wavy
and black as a raven.
His eyes are like doves
by the water streams,
washed in milk,
mounted like jewels.
His cheeks are like beds of spice
yielding perfume.
His lips are like lilies
dripping with myrrh.
His arms are rods of gold
set with chrysolite.
His body is like polished ivory
decorated with sapphires.
His legs are pillars of marble
set on bases of pure gold.
His appearance is like Lebanon,
choice as its cedars.
His mouth is sweetness itself;
he is altogether lovely.
This is my lover, this my friend,
O daughters of Jerusalem. (Song of Songs 5:1-2, 8-16)

3. Why do you suppose passages like this are in the Bible?

4. How would you change the beloved's descriptions of her lover's head, hair, eyes, cheeks, lips, arms, body, legs, appearance, and mouth to fit our culture and time?

5. If you wrote a note like this to your spouse, what do you think would be his or her reaction?

Applying the Principles

According to the Rosbergs, wives are especially interested in non-sexual touch, romance, and spiritual intimacy. Husbands want mutual satisfaction, responsiveness, and initiation.

Here are six "surprise packages" containing these actions and qualities. Try ranking them from 1 to 6 (1 being highest) in the following areas:

- how surprised you think your spouse would be to receive them
- which would be most appreciated
- which would be most costly in terms of time and effort
- which you would most like to receive

If you can, get your spouse's reaction to your rankings. Then, pick what you believe is your spouse's most desired gift of the six—without telling him or her what it is. Plan how and when you'll present that gift this week.

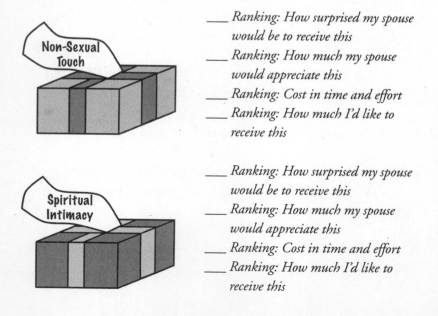

Non-Sexual Touch

___ *Ranking: How surprised my spouse would be to receive this*
___ *Ranking: How much my spouse would appreciate this*
___ *Ranking: Cost in time and effort*
___ *Ranking: How much I'd like to receive this*

Spiritual Intimacy

___ *Ranking: How surprised my spouse would be to receive this*
___ *Ranking: How much my spouse would appreciate this*
___ *Ranking: Cost in time and effort*
___ *Ranking: How much I'd like to receive this*

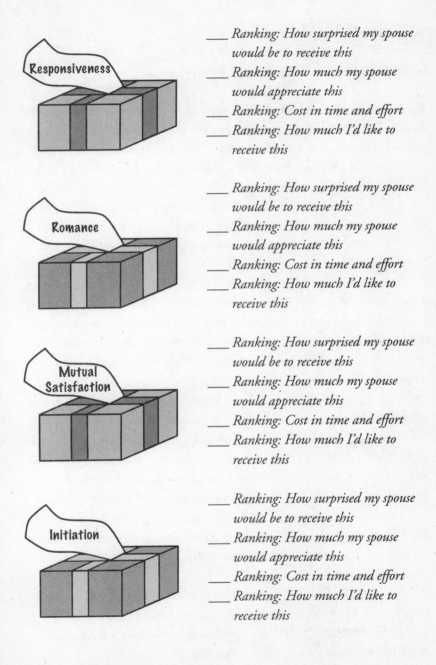

Responsiveness

___ *Ranking: How surprised my spouse would be to receive this*
___ *Ranking: How much my spouse would appreciate this*
___ *Ranking: Cost in time and effort*
___ *Ranking: How much I'd like to receive this*

Romance

___ *Ranking: How surprised my spouse would be to receive this*
___ *Ranking: How much my spouse would appreciate this*
___ *Ranking: Cost in time and effort*
___ *Ranking: How much I'd like to receive this*

Mutual Satisfaction

___ *Ranking: How surprised my spouse would be to receive this*
___ *Ranking: How much my spouse would appreciate this*
___ *Ranking: Cost in time and effort*
___ *Ranking: How much I'd like to receive this*

Initiation

___ *Ranking: How surprised my spouse would be to receive this*
___ *Ranking: How much my spouse would appreciate this*
___ *Ranking: Cost in time and effort*
___ *Ranking: How much I'd like to receive this*

Encouragement from a Counselor

Many couples learn to their chagrin that sexual arousal is a very individual matter. One spouse wants the lights on; the other wants it dark. Each partner prefers a certain touch, a certain time, even a certain temperature.

When you and your mate like "different strokes," what should you do? Here are five suggestions.

1. *Discover your comfort zone.* You probably would expect to negotiate which colors to paint the rooms of your new house, or whether to serve tofu for dinner. Why be surprised if you encounter some differences in your sexual desires?

Some argue that this process could be helped along by living together before the wedding. But statistics prove otherwise. Studies reveal that, instead of increasing sexual compatibility, premarital cohabitation actually boosts the likelihood of sexually transmitted disease, sexual dysfunction, codependency, divorce, and loss of trust. Clearly, becoming one flesh is sacred for a reason.

2. *Be a servant.* Your approach to sex should mirror your approach to marriage in general: "Serve one another in love" (Galatians 5:13).

Solomon referred to his wife as "my sister, my bride" (Song of Solomon 4:10). Can you keep the perspective of being brother and sister in Christ as well as being spouses? A servant's attitude can guard against letting differences in bed become a power struggle or cause for resentment.

Basic issues of preference, such as whether to have the lights on, are good opportunities to listen and learn what pleases your spouse. If something causes one partner embarrassment or discomfort, he or she should never feel pressured to participate.

3. *Discern moral issues.* Each of us enters marriage with an "arousal template" or set of stimuli that triggers sexual interest. If you've had prior sexual relationships or exposure to pornography, for example, unhealthy appetites may have been added to your template.

Even between consenting spouses, certain sexual behaviors are still wrong. For example, a husband may claim that pornography helps his sex life—but its use actually constitutes an act of adultery (Matthew 5:27-28). Any sexual practices that are demeaning or physically harmful will damage true intimacy as well as violating biblical guidelines. Work together to find *what's* right instead of fighting over *who's* right.

4. *Address trauma or addiction.* If conflict over sex escalates beyond simply choosing a "menu" you both like, it's possible there's a history of sexual trauma for one or both spouses. Associating shame or fear with sexuality is a powerful dynamic to overcome. Survivors of childhood sexual abuse, for example, often need the help of a professional Christian counselor to restore a healthy sex life.

5. *Talk about sex.* No matter what your sexual differences are, the first step to connecting well sexually is to do so verbally. Sometimes discussing these issues during intimacy can evoke feelings of shame or embarrassment. So it's often a good idea to wait and discuss it later, outside the bedroom.

Let's get back to Jill and Mark. Jill's still standing there with the gift of lingerie. What should she do?

Mark hesitates, seeing her expression. "I—I hope I didn't shock you with the present," he stammers. "I know it's not your usual style, but I really thought you'd look beautiful in it."

Jill smooths the gold ribbon on the box. She starts thinking about how Mark has shown her in so many ways that she is God's gift to him.

A shy smile plays across her lips. She even quits worrying about how her thighs would look in this outfit.

Okay, she thinks. *As long as he treasures me like this, I'll wrap his gift any way he likes.*

—Rob Jackson
Licensed Professional Counselor[4]

FLAMMABLE

Chapter 3

GREAT SEX IN A GODLY MARRIAGE (PART 2)

Lisa and Tom had been married two and a half years when Lisa set up an appointment for them to see a counselor.

"Tell me what you'd like to work on in therapy," the counselor said.

"Our sex life," Lisa answered.

"Yeah," Tom added. "She never wants to do it, and I'm getting tired of waiting. My friends are doing it three to five times a week. And, man, I'm lucky if I get it once!"

"Lisa," the therapist said, "tell me what's going on from your perspective."

"Well, it's not like I thought it would be. . . . I just thought it would be a lot more fun."

"She just does it because she has to," Tom declared. "Not because she wants to. And I don't know why she doesn't want to."

Lisa looked up, suddenly finding her voice. "You are so careless and selfish!" she cried. "We used to talk. We used to kiss. Now whenever you reach for me I know there's just one thing on your mind—sex."

"Okay," the therapist said, intervening. "How much time do you guys spend when you make love?"

"Oh, about 10 minutes," said Tom.

"Well, that could be a big part of the problem," said the therapist.

When it comes to sex, many married couples wonder whether they're "doing it right"—especially if, like Lisa and Tom, they find themselves dissatisfied with the way things are going.

There are a number of factors that contribute to whether your sexual intimacy is satisfying. "Doing it right" is just one of them.

—Sandra Lundberg
Licensed Psychologist[5]

Identifying Your Needs

Take a couple of minutes to fill out the following survey.

1. If you needed advice about sex, where would you go? Why?
   ____ the Internet
   ____ a marriage counselor
   ____ a sex therapist
   ____ a pastor
   ____ a book
   ____ other _____

2. Which of the following is most like your love life these days?
   ____ The Discovery Channel
   ____ The History Channel
   ____ MTV
   ____ Comedy Central
   ____ other _____

3. Which of the following do you think would result in the biggest improvement in most married people's sexual lives?

___ if men were more like women

___ if women were more like men

___ if everybody became a Christian

___ if the electricity went off after 9:00 P.M. every night

___ if pornographers went out of business

___ if everyone joined a health club

___ other _____

4. In 25 words or less, how would you summarize what the Bible says about sexuality? _____

_____

5. Do you think the way to a man's heart is through his stomach? Why or why not? What do you think is the way to a woman's heart?

_____

6. Do you think those with a strong faith have better sexual relationships in their marriages than others do? Why or why not? _____

_____

Watching and Discussing the DVD

Ready for some straight talk from authors Kay Arthur and Dr. Juli Slattery?

In this video segment, Kay challenges us to take a biblical view of God's good gift of sexuality, swimming against the cultural current that excuses infidelity and short-term wedlock. Juli, a psychologist, is frank and funny as she tackles the question of how real couples—even parents of little kids—can have sex lives. How can you find time to be intimate?

What if you don't feel attractive? How can you get your spouse more interested in sex?

If you sometimes find physical intimacy to be more of a minefield than a mountaintop experience, this session is for you.

After viewing the DVD, use questions like these to help you think through what you saw and heard.

1. Which of the following comes closest to describing your response to this DVD segment? Why?
    - Let's move on to a less embarrassing subject.
    - It gave me a lot to think about.
    - It needed more guys.
    - It gave me hope.
    - other _____

2. Does it matter to you what the "biblical view of sexuality" is? If so, could you prove in court how much it matters to you? Why or why not?

3. How would you describe Kay Arthur's approach to sexuality? How do you think the following people would describe it? Why?
    - the characters on TV shows like *Friends* and *Two and a Half Men*
    - Christians of the past like Martin Luther and John Bunyan
    - contemporary Christians in Africa
    - American Christians 20 years from now

4. Kay points out that God designed sex, that it's good and beautiful and bonds spouses together. How could you try to convince the following people of that fact?
    - a husband who grew up hearing in church that sex is dirty
    - a wife who was sexually abused as a child

- a husband who believes sex is just a matter of hormones and instinct
- a wife who finds sex boring and unfulfilling

5. Dr. Juli Slattery notes that in one survey more than 80 percent of husbands said their fondest desire was that their wives would initiate sex more often. Does this surprise you? Why or why not?

6. According to Juli, a wife wants to know that her husband doesn't just want to have sex, but wants to have sex with her. How can a husband make this clear to his wife?

7. Juli points out the importance of telling your spouse about your need for physical intimacy. What do you think is the best time of day to do this? The best place? Why?

Bible Study

> *"Everything is permissible for me"—but not everything is beneficial. "Everything is permissible for me"—but I will not be mastered by anything. "Food for the stomach and the stomach for food"—but God will destroy them both. The body is not meant for sexual immorality, but for the Lord, and the Lord for the body. By his power God raised the Lord from the dead, and he will raise us also. Do you not know that your bodies are members of Christ himself? Shall I then take the members of Christ and unite them with a prostitute? Never! Do you not know that he who unites himself with a prostitute is one with her in body? For it is said, "The two will become one flesh." But he who unites himself with the Lord is one with him in spirit.*

Flee from sexual immorality. All other sins a man commits are out-side his body, but he who sins sexually sins against his own body. Do you not know that your body is a temple of the Holy Spirit, who is in you, whom you have received from God? You are not your own; you were bought at a price. Therefore honor God with your body. (1 Corinthians 6:12-20)

1. If sexuality is God-given, good, and beautiful, why are all these warnings necessary?

2. Which verse in 1 Corinthians 6:12-20 do you think would be most controversial in our society today? Why?

Now for the matters you wrote about: It is good for a man not to marry. But since there is so much immorality, each man should have his own wife, and each woman her own husband. The husband should ful-fill his marital duty to his wife, and likewise the wife to her husband. The wife's body does not belong to her alone but also to her husband. In the same way, the husband's body does not belong to him alone but also to his wife. Do not deprive each other except by mutual consent and for a time, so that you may devote yourselves to prayer. Then come to-gether again so that Satan will not tempt you because of your lack of self-control. I say this as a concession, not as a command. I wish that all men were as I am. But each man has his own gift from God; one has this gift, another has that. (1 Corinthians 7:1-7)

3. If marriage is God-given, good, and beautiful, why did Paul say it was good to stay single?

4. Does "marital duty" refer only to sex? Does it imply that sex is a chore? Why or why not?

5. Which verse in Corinthians 7:1-7 do you think would be most controversial in our society today? Why?

> *If a man has recently married, he must not be sent to war or have any other duty laid on him. For one year he is to be free to stay at home and bring happiness to the wife he has married. (Deuteronomy 24:5)*

6. Why do you suppose this rule was included in the Bible? What does it tell you about God's attitude toward the pleasurable aspects of marriage?

7. Does a husband's responsibility to bring his wife happiness end after the first year? How do you know? Does this apply to the wife as well? Why or why not?

Applying the Principles

Remember these suggestions for wives from the DVD?
- Look good, and wear good-looking clothes.
- Save some energy for the end of the day and spend it on your husband.
- Believe your husband when he tells you you're beautiful.
- Build up and encourage your husband in other, non-sexual areas.

How about these suggestions for husbands?
- Be satisfied with your wife, including her body.
- Tell your wife how important sex—with her—is to you.
- Take your wife on a date or give her a gift.
- Offer to do a chore for her or give her a back rub.

Pick two suggestions from those that apply to you. Then circle all the things on the following list that make it hard for you to do those two things:

- I can't compete with the "beautiful" people on TV and in the movies.
- It costs too much money.
- My schedule is crazy.
- I'm shy.
- I don't feel good about the way I look.
- I've gotten out of the habit of paying attention to my spouse.
- I'm afraid my spouse will reject me.
- It's easier to be negative than positive.
- I'm afraid my spouse won't believe me.
- I'm too tired.
- I'd be embarrassed.
- other _____

If you're comfortable doing so, pray with your spouse about the obstacles you circled. Finally, plan to follow through this week on the easier of the two suggestions you chose.

Encouragement from a Counselor

A good sexual relationship has a lot to do with how the two of you are doing *outside* the bedroom. If you're having problems with sexual intimacy, you're probably having trouble in other areas as well. This can be an indicator that you need to work on your relationship.

Establishing a solid sexual relationship in your marriage should be a goal the two of you share. To attain that goal, your sexual experiences need to be satisfying for both of you. Here are a few keys to finding that satisfaction—keys that show "doing it right" is about more than technique.

1. *Take care of your body.* Regular exercise, good nutrition, and good hygiene are just as important now that you're married as they were when you were single. During your dating days you most likely presented your best self to each other—showered, shaved, powdered, and perfumed. Married couples often get lazy about these things. But if you don't want to be taken for granted—much less avoided—maintain those good grooming habits that contributed to your attraction to one another.

2. *Be upfront.* Each of you needs to take responsibility for whether or not your sex life is satisfying. Tell your spouse what feels good to you and what you need; don't assume he or she will "just know." Your spouse can't read your mind. As for faking satisfaction—that will only hurt both of you, damaging mutual trust and guaranteeing that you won't get your needs met. So figure out what you need and go for it.

3. *Plan ahead.* Make your sexual relationship a priority. You may need to schedule blocks of time to be physical together, times when you won't let other things interrupt. Scheduling sex may at first seem contrived and unnatural. Yet you may find that it leads to better sexual experiences for the two of you, thereby improving the quality of your marriage.

4. *Take the time.* Plan special days and moments together. Make them romantic. For some couples this comes naturally; for others sex has become repetitive and boring, and kicking stale habits takes extra effort. Make time to talk about your sexual relationship—preferably when you're not in the middle of a sexual encounter. Take time with sexual activity itself, remembering the hugging, kissing, and caressing the two of you probably enjoyed before marriage.

5. *Give yourselves a break.* Your sexual times together need to be free of demands, and from any anxiety associated with that. Replace those stressors with closeness, warmth, pleasure, and fun. You'll be more likely

to "lose yourself" in your spouse and the feelings you're enjoying together.

6. *Deal with scars and habits.* Real intimacy can be difficult to achieve if you're carrying around the baggage of sexual abuse, premarital sexual relations, or pornography use. If one of these is an issue for either of you, it's an issue for both of you. Don't wait to get help. There are trained Christian therapists who can assist you.

After their first appointment with the therapist, Lisa and Tom had a lot to talk about.

"I didn't know my going fast was making you feel so bad," Tom said. "I thought it would take the pressure off you if I just got it over with."

Lisa shook her head. "I don't want to just get it over with! Well, sometimes I do. But mostly that makes me feel used. I just want it to be like it used to be, when we'd spend hours just hanging out, talking, laughing. I never thought it would be like this."

"So you think we need to go see the therapist again?" Tom asked.

"Absolutely."

In terms of rebuilding a fulfilling sexual relationship, Lisa and Tom were finally doing it right.

—Sandra Lundberg
Licensed Psychologist[6]

Chapter 4

EXPRESSING YOUR ANGER THE RIGHT WAY

Once again, Sue and Ken have gone to bed angry. Each lies as far over on his or her side of the bed as is humanly possible.

Sue is thinking about the terrible things Ken said to her, and how afraid she was. She'll spend most of the night unable to sleep, remembering all their fights in almost three years of marriage.

Ken, meanwhile, is exhausted. He thinks about how unreasonable Sue is. Then, suddenly, he falls asleep.

Some couples, like Ken and Sue, have a habit of letting arguments get out of control. Others find it happening only once in a while. Still others try never to raise any sensitive subjects, fearing the resulting argument will degenerate into a verbal battle that leads inevitably to divorce.

Why do arguments spin out of control? And how can anger be expressed in a healthy marriage?

—Romie Hurley
Licensed Professional Counselor[7]

Identifying Your Needs

Here's a survey; please take a few minutes to fill it out.

1. In your opinion, which of the following words describe anger? Why?
   ___ dangerous
   ___ cleansing
   ___ sinful
   ___ righteous
   ___ normal
   ___ exhausting

2. Which of the following do you think Jesus might say about anger? Why?
   ___ "You have heard it said that fighting is evil; I tell you that anyone who grows angry will not inherit the kingdom of heaven."
   ___ "Blessed are those who are angry for My sake."
   ___ "The anger of man is of no consequence to God."
   ___ "Be angry as I am angry."
   ___ "If you are angry at another, you are angry at Me."

3. Rank the following in order to show how angry you think each situation would make your spouse—from most to least upset.
   ___ You ate a piece of the cake your spouse was saving for a party at work.
   ___ You accidentally sat on your spouse's eyeglasses and broke them.
   ___ You forgot to pay the electric bill, and the power to your home has been shut off.

___ You made a joke about your spouse's weight in front of friends.

___ You're having an affair.

___ You're 30 minutes late getting ready for church.

4. If anger were furniture, what would your living room look like? Would it be crowded? Would the furniture be old or new?

_____

5. If you had to rewrite your wedding vows to include a statement about anger, what would it be? _____

_____

6. Is there any way in which anger could help a marriage? If so, what might it be? If not, why not? _____

_____

Watching and Discussing the DVD

Is it possible to have marriage without anger? Yes, if both spouses are robots!

For the rest of us, this DVD segment examines how anger affects *human* couples—and how they can keep it from eating away at their relationship. Family coaches Dr. Gary and Barb Rosberg team up with psychologist and educator Dr. Archibald Hart to explain how to keep this powerful emotion from turning into rage or revenge. Host Dr. Greg Smalley shares a down-to-earth story on the subject, too.

Every marriage has anger; find out how to manage it instead of letting it manage you.

After viewing the DVD, use questions like these to help you think through what you saw and heard.

1. If you and your spouse were guests on a TV psychologist's show, which of the following might be the title of that episode? Why?
   - "Spouses Who Throw Things, and the Dishes They've Broken"
   - "Spouses Who Argue, and the Pets Who Avoid Them"
   - "Spouses Who Clam Up, and the Silence That's Deafening"
   - other _____

2. Dr. Gary and Barb Rosberg say they've met many Christians who don't think anger is a God-given emotion. What might these people believe instead?

3. How could anger play a positive role in each of the following situations?
   - During an argument, your spouse blurts out that your spending on clothes is higher than the mortgage payment.
   - You and your spouse get mad when you learn that a neighbor is endangering her children by using a kerosene heater in her house.
   - Your spouse threatens to call the doctor if you don't start taking your blood pressure medication regularly.
   - When your spouse refuses to see a marriage counselor with you, you're so angry you decide to see a counselor on your own.

4. The Rosbergs note that spouses may get angry when they're criticized. Why are the following not good ways to deal with that? Why? What would be a better strategy?

- Never criticize your spouse.
- Deliver all your criticism in the form of anonymous letters.
- Preface your criticism with, "I know you think you're perfect, but . . ."
- When your spouse reacts angrily, say, "I knew you'd do that."

5. Dr. Archibald Hart has said that anger is like a smoke alarm; it tells you that something's wrong and you need to figure out what it is. In your home, what kinds of things tend to set off the alarm?
   - annoying habits
   - lack of communication
   - conflict over money, chores, in-laws, or sex
   - differences in parenting
   - other _____

6. What's your usual response when the "smoke alarm" of anger goes off in your home? How do you feel about that?
   - I panic and call the "fire department."
   - I take out the "battery" to make the noise stop.
   - I make sure everybody is safe and look for the source of the smoke.
   - other _____

7. Dr. Hart suggests several steps to take when you feel angry at your spouse. Which of these are hardest for you? Why?
   - Acknowledge that you feel angry and reflect on that.
   - Gain control of yourself.
   - Take a "time out" if necessary to slow things down.
   - Take responsibility for your feelings.
   - If you said something inappropriate, apologize immediately.

8. According to Dr. Hart, forgiveness is the best antidote to anger. What happens if you refuse to give that antidote to your spouse?

Bible Study

A fool shows his annoyance at once, but a prudent man overlooks an insult. . . . A fool gives full vent to his anger, but a wise man keeps himself under control. (Proverbs 12:16; 29:11)

1. What do you conclude about anger from these proverbs?
   ____ It's a sin.
   ____ It's powerful.
   ____ You should resist it.
   ____ You should resist expressing it.
   ____ other _____

For as churning the milk produces butter, and as twisting the nose produces blood, so stirring up anger produces strife. (Proverbs 30:33)

2. Have you ever stirred up anger in your marriage by doing one of the following things? Would you recommend that to other couples? Why or why not?
   ____ bringing up an old conflict that hasn't been resolved
   ____ criticizing your in-laws
   ____ asking why your spouse isn't more like your mother or father
   ____ breaking a promise

EXPRESSING YOUR ANGER THE RIGHT WAY   43

____ teasing your spouse about a subject you know is "sensitive"

"In your anger do not sin": Do not let the sun go down while you are still angry. (Ephesians 4:26)

3. When does anger become sin? How does dealing with anger quickly keep it from turning into sin? What usually happens if you and your spouse don't address anger within 24 hours?

For man's anger does not bring about the righteous life that God desires. (James 1:20)

4. Which of the following do you think are examples of James 1:20 in action? Why?

____ A wife threatens to leave her husband unless he goes with her to a marriage counselor.

____ A husband demands that his wife follow his "spiritual leadership."

____ A husband shoves his wife during an argument.

____ A wife discovers pornography on her husband's computer and throws the machine in the garbage.

____ other _____

[Love] is not rude, it is not self-seeking, it is not easily angered, it keeps no record of wrongs. (1 Corinthians 13:5)

5. What does rudeness have to do with anger? What's the difference between getting angry and being easily angered? In a marriage, how does anger often lead to keeping a record of wrongs—and vice versa? How could not keeping such a record reduce the level of anger in a marriage?

Applying the Principles

Dr. Archibald Hart suggests giving your spouse a signal when he or she seems angry. How might it help? What should the signal be? What would be a healthy response to such a signal?

To help you start discussing this with your spouse, here's a diagram. Draw a star wherever you think your spouse tends to display symptoms of anger (see the list for ideas). Then draw an "X" wherever you tend to feel anger yourself.

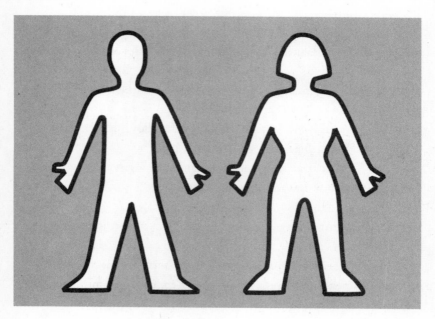

Some possible symptoms of anger:
- Muscles tense.
- Voice gets louder, quieter, higher, lower, or strained.
- Eyes narrow, close, or look away.

- Frown appears.
- Fists clench.
- Body stiffens.
- Stomach becomes upset.
- Heart beats faster.
- Brow furrows.
- Arms fold.
- Chin is raised.
- Sighing or throat-clearing occurs.
- Legs cross.
- Foot taps.

After showing your diagrams to your spouse and talking about how accurate you think they are, consider asking each other for permission to give a signal when you see (or feel) those symptoms. Take a moment to choose what the signal should be.

Encouragement from a Counselor

Here are seven things couples need to understand about disagreements that go off the deep end.

1. Spouses become irrational for many reasons. It can stem from feeling overwhelmed, threatened, provoked, criticized, or just misunderstood. The emotions may not be wrong, but their out-of-control expression can be. As the Bible says, "A fool gives full vent to his anger, but a wise man keeps himself under control" (Proverbs 29:11).

2. Some people seem only too glad to lose control during an argument. There's a kind of adrenaline rush that comes with expressing anger, and it can be addictive.

3. Fearing out-of-control arguments can cause a spouse to bury his or her feelings, so as not to provoke the other person. That may work in the short run, but ignoring explosive issues won't work long-term. They'll eventually come to a head.

4. A wife tends to remember situations much longer than a husband does, and the danger of her dredging up the past is not only real but common. This is overwhelming to the spouse who tends to forget, or wants to forget, things said and done in anger.

5. Both aggressive and passive/aggressive behavior can be dangerous. In most couples, one spouse tends to be more of an aggressive pursuer in arguments. This person usually gets more of the blame because he or she is easy to identify. But the passive, quieter mate who nags or blames is often just as destructive.

6. Bullying in a relationship can be intimidating, but it's important not to run from threats. It's better to find a constructive way to deal with the bullying and avoid living in fear. There are times when a gentle spirit can turn away wrath (Proverbs 15:1), but this is presented in the Bible as an intentional, positive act—not one motivated by fear of provoking someone to anger.

7. Physical violence is never okay. Threats of physical violence must be handled immediately. If you feel threatened, get to a safe place. Put distance between you and the person endangering you; call the police if necessary.

Physical violence doesn't stop without intervention. Abusers must learn to manage anger. Once the danger is past, insist on counseling. Also, educate yourself about abuse cycles and how to protect yourself in the future.

No matter how much you and your spouse love each other, no matter how understanding you try to be, and no matter how strongly you want to avoid hurting each other, there will be times when arguments get out of control. Here are some ways to prepare for those times and to minimize their negative effects.

1. Be aware of your physical reactions and triggers, to let you know when it's time to back off. Most people tense up when uncomfortable or threatened.

2. Take responsibility to communicate how you're feeling and what you're thinking.

3. Never, ever bully, threaten, or intimidate your spouse.

4. Ask for a time-out when you need it; set another time to talk.

5. If you know a subject is too volatile to handle alone, discuss it in the presence of a neutral party such as a pastor or counselor.

6. If you're "walking on eggshells" or hiding in fear in order to avoid angering your spouse, get outside help.

7. Pray with your spouse when things get too intense, even if you avoid the immediate topic for the moment. The act of submitting to God's authority may bring some relief.

8. Pray individually—a prayer of repentance for your own attitude and actions.

9. Forgive your spouse. This doesn't mean agreeing with his or her position or excusing abuse; it means giving up your determination to get revenge.

Don't let your anger, or your spouse's, dominate your relationship. And don't let fear of an out-of-control argument keep you and your mate from communicating honestly.

—Romie Hurley
Licensed Professional Counselor[8]

Chapter 5

DEALING WITH DEPRESSION TOGETHER

Clint has always been somewhat up and down emotionally—sometimes on a "high" and sometimes subdued—especially compared to Julie, his even-tempered wife. Over the last two or three months, however, it's become increasingly obvious to Julie that her husband is descending into blacker and blacker moods.

Clint denies that he's depressed, believing he's just reacting to things that aren't going well at work. He sees no reason to consider consulting a counselor. He has no idea that he may be suffering from a bipolar disorder that requires medication and therapy if it's not to become even more pronounced.

Then there's Andrea, who's just given birth to her first child. Suddenly she's irrational, in the pits of despair at a time when she's "supposed" to be filled with joy. Ashamed, she tries desperately to hide her feelings—which include the sensation that she's "going crazy."

Andrea has thoughts that the rest of her family might be better off without her. She's seriously considering suicide, even thinking she'll take the new baby with her. Neither she nor her husband knows she's suffering from postpartum depression, which can be successfully treated when properly diagnosed.

What can Clint's and Andrea's spouses do?

—Phillip J. Swihart
Clinical Psychologist[9]

Identifying Your Needs

Here are some questions to help you start thinking about the topic of this session.

1. Which of the following words or phrases come to mind when you hear the word depression? Why?

   ____ sad

   ____ weak

   ____ stock market crash

   ____ darkness

   ____ dent

   ____ other _____

2. How do you think a depressed spouse would react to each of the following situations?

   • gaining 15 pounds

   _____

   • never hearing a compliment from his or her spouse

   _____

   • winning a new car

   _____

   • a sermon titled "Living in the Joy of the Lord"

   _____

   • losing his or her job

   _____

   • a spouse who says, "Let's go away for the weekend"

   _____

3. Which of the following do you think cause depression? Why?

____ a chemical imbalance

____ lack of faith

____ stress

___ self-centeredness

___ exhaustion

___ disappointment

___ other _____

4. How can you tell whether your spouse is depressed?

_____

5. If you were depressed, who would you tell about it? Why?

_____

6. If you were depressed, how do you think your spouse would respond?

_____

Watching and Discussing the DVD

You won't find any ivory-tower platitudes in this video segment. Three counselors—Mitch Temple, Dr. Gary Rosberg, and Dr. Juli Slattery—tell the unvarnished truth about their own battles with depression.

Any spouse can be hit with a job loss, the death of a loved one, a chemical imbalance, postpartum stress, or other circumstance that spirals downward into hopelessness. What if it's you? What if it's your husband or wife?

Depression can destroy a relationship. In this session, the experts explain what helped them—and their marriages—survive.

After viewing the DVD, use questions like these to help you think through what you saw and heard.

1. What was your attitude toward depression before you watched this DVD segment? Did it change at all? If so, how? If not, why not?

2. Which of the following symptoms of depression were mentioned in this video? How might someone first notice them in a spouse? Which ones would be easiest to ignore or dismiss? Why?
   - fatigue
   - weight loss or gain
   - mood swings
   - suicidal thoughts
   - difficulty sleeping
   - lack of concentration
   - crying spells
   - intense sadness or self-doubt
   - inability to enjoy favorite activities

3. How did Mitch Temple's depression affect his wife and children? Why was it still hard for him to see that he was depressed and to get the help he needed? On a scale of 1 to 10 (10 hardest), how difficult would it be for you to admit you were depressed? Why?

4. How did Mitch's wife contribute to his recovery? If you were depressed, how would you want your spouse to help you?

5. What loss led to Dr. Gary Rosberg's depression? How was it different from normal grieving?

6. Barb Rosberg prayed that God would change the circumstances of her husband's life—but He didn't. What would you have done at that point? What did Barb do, and what was the result?

7. Dr. Juli Slattery says that depression affects the way spouses communicate and the way they see each other. How would you expect a depressed person to communicate with and see his or her spouse? How would you expect the spouse to communicate with and see the depressed person?

8. If you had encountered Juli at church during her postpartum depression and asked, "How are you?" what do you think she would have replied? Why? How can a person make it easier for his or her spouse to be honest about being depressed?

Bible Study

Now Ahab told Jezebel everything Elijah had done and how he had killed all the prophets with the sword. So Jezebel sent a messenger to Elijah to say, "May the gods deal with me, be it ever so severely, if by this time tomorrow I do not make your life like that of one of them."

Elijah was afraid and ran for his life. When he came to Beersheba in Judah, he left his servant there, while he himself went a day's journey into the desert. He came to a broom tree, sat down under it and prayed that he might die. "I have had enough, LORD," he said. "Take my life; I am no better than my ancestors." Then he lay down under the tree and fell asleep.

All at once an angel touched him and said, "Get up and eat." He looked around, and there by his head was a cake of bread baked over hot coals, and a jar of water. He ate and drank and then lay down again.

The angel of the LORD came back a second time and touched him and said, "Get up and eat, for the journey is too much for you." So he got up and ate and drank. Strengthened by that food, he traveled forty days and forty nights until he reached Horeb, the mountain of God. There he went into a cave and spent the night.

And the word of the LORD came to him: "What are you doing here, Elijah?"

He replied, "I have been very zealous for the LORD God Almighty. The Israelites have rejected your covenant, broken down your altars, and put your prophets to death with the sword. I am the only one left, and now they are trying to kill me too."

The LORD said, "Go out and stand on the mountain in the presence of the LORD, for the LORD is about to pass by."

Then a great and powerful wind tore the mountains apart and shattered the rocks before the LORD, but the LORD was not in the wind. After the wind there was an earthquake, but the LORD was not in the earthquake. After the earthquake came a fire, but the LORD was not in the fire. And after the fire came a gentle whisper. When Elijah heard it, he pulled his cloak over his face and went out and stood at the mouth of the cave.

Then a voice said to him, "What are you doing here, Elijah?"

He replied, "I have been very zealous for the LORD God Almighty. The Israelites have rejected your covenant, broken down your altars, and put your prophets to death with the sword. I am the only one left, and now they are trying to kill me too."

The LORD said to him, "Go back the way you came, and go to the Desert of Damascus. When you get there, anoint Hazael king over Aram. Also, anoint Jehu son of Nimshi king over Israel, and anoint Elisha son of Shaphat from Abel Meholah to succeed you as prophet. Jehu will put to death any who escape the sword of Hazael, and Elisha will put to death any who escape the sword of Jehu. Yet I reserve seven thousand in Israel— all whose knees have not bowed down to Baal and all whose mouths have not kissed him." (1 Kings 19:1-18)

1. What symptoms of depression did Elijah have? What "treatment" did the angel and the Lord provide? How might a husband or wife do something similar for a depressed spouse?

Then Job replied:

"How long will you torment me and crush me with words?

Ten times now you have reproached me; shamelessly you attack me.

If it is true that I have gone astray, my error remains my concern alone.

If indeed you would exalt yourselves above me and use my humiliation against me, then know that God has wronged me and drawn his net around me.

"Though I cry, 'I've been wronged!' I get no response; though I call for help, there is no justice.

He has blocked my way so I cannot pass; he has shrouded my paths in darkness. (Job 19:1-8)

2. How might this speech be worded if Job's situation had been one of the following? What would you do in each case if Job were your spouse?
   - if Job had lost his job a year before and hadn't been able to find a new one
   - if Job had just learned that he had multiple sclerosis
   - if Job had been imprisoned for a crime he didn't commit
   - if Job had just lost his six-year-old son in a car accident

My tears have been my food day and night, while men say to me all day long, "Where is your God?"

These things I remember as I pour out my soul: how I used to go with the multitude, leading the procession to the house of God, with shouts of joy and thanksgiving among the festive throng.

Why are you downcast, O my soul?

Why so disturbed within me?

Put your hope in God,

for I will yet praise him,

my Savior and my God.

My soul is downcast within me;
therefore I will remember you
from the land of the Jordan,
the heights of Hermon—from Mount Mizar. (Psalm 42:3-6)

3. Would you say that the psalmist was depressed? Why or why not?
   What does he suggest as the solution? What might have happened if
   the psalmist's wife had bought a greeting card with this message on it
   and had given it to him?

Applying the Principles

Which of the following do you most need to do this week?
- find out whether your spouse is depressed
- prepare for a future time when your spouse might be depressed
- let your spouse know that you're depressed
- help your spouse get treatment for depression
- get a break from being around your depressed spouse
- other _____

As a first step toward achieving the goal you just chose, try writing
your spouse a note designed to do one or more of the following:
- Ask whether your spouse might be depressed, noting symptoms
  you've observed.
- Promise to be supportive if he or she is—or ever becomes—
  depressed.
- Let your spouse know that you're depressed.
- Offer to help your spouse get treatment for depression.
- Share the most important principle you learned in this session.

If you need guidance on living with a depressed spouse and would like to speak with a therapist, Focus on the Family maintains a referral network of Christian counselors. For information, call 1-800-A-FAMILY and ask for the counseling department.

Encouragement from a Counselor

When does your mate need psychological help?

Certainly some symptoms are unambiguous. Is he abusing you or your children? Has she quit eating and her loss of weight is possibly life-threatening? Is he hearing voices no one else hears, or seeing things no one else sees? Is she saying she no longer wants to live?

In situations like these, when issues of safety are involved for you or your spouse or your children, arrange immediate intervention. If your children clearly are at risk, it's your responsibility as the rational spouse to take whatever measures are needed to protect them.

Ask a Christian therapist in your area how you can accomplish such intervention quickly and appropriately. If you're in a life-threatening crisis, call 911 and ask law enforcement to act.

In most cases symptoms of emotional problems are much less dramatic. Sometimes they're so subtle that neither spouse recognizes how serious they're becoming.

You can look for a number of other symptoms which may indicate that your spouse needs help from a professional Christian therapist. These include deviations from that person's normal behaviors—things that are out of character for him or her. If your spouse's personality seems to be changing in a negative way, that can be a red flag.

A string of significant losses also can damage mental health. Death of parents or children, loss of a job, financial reverses, serious medical problems—all can contribute to a major psychological crisis that builds over time.

But what if your spouse has little or no insight into his or her feelings and behaviors? What if he or she rejects the idea of counseling?

You might begin by suggesting that your spouse see your family physician for a thorough physical and possibly lab tests. This is often less threatening than pushing the notion of therapy, which can result in protests like, "You think I'm crazy!" and "You think I need a shrink!"

Such an approach is also valuable in ruling out other possible causes for some symptoms. Diabetics and those suffering from thyroid disorders may also experience mood swings, for example.

In addition, a physician knowledgeable about psychiatric disorders may be able to convince a defensive spouse that he or she does indeed need psychological help. The doctor can then make an appropriate referral.

Finally, it's also important to understand that a spouse with symptoms of emotional distress may have a spiritual problem that hasn't been recognized or addressed.

For example, unconfessed sin with its accompanying guilt can wreak havoc on a person's psychological well-being. Emotional distress due to the need to submit to God's will can be a good thing; it may serve as a siren of spiritual danger.

In such cases, counseling with a pastor or other spiritual mentor as well as a Christian therapist may be useful. It can help the person face himself or herself, to be honest about his or her rebellion and poor choices, and to seek spiritual restoration.

—Phillip J. Swihart
Clinical Psychologist[10]

Chapter 6

THE WONDERFUL WORLD OF FINANCES

When Teri and Phil came into the counselor's office, they were in crisis.

They'd brought debt into their marriage, but had never had a handle on how to reduce it. Now they were spending several hundred dollars a month more than they made. Not having a budget, they didn't even know where their money was going. They didn't have enough cash to do anything for themselves or their three children.

As a result, their marriage was in trouble. They barely spoke to each other.

Knowing how much you can spend is vital to the health of your relationship as well as your bank account. But deciding how much that is may not be a simple matter.

For one thing, people enter marriage with different patterns of spending, saving, and giving. Trying to merge two systems often leads to conflict. Karl and Trina, for instance, grew up in families that took different positions on whether it's okay for Christians to borrow money. Karl believes it's fine to take out a loan for a car. Trina doesn't agree; she thinks cars should be paid for with cash.

You and your spouse need to agree on your spending habits, which means coming up with a plan of compromise that you're both comfortable with.

How can you do that?

—Sandra Lundberg
Licensed Psychologist[11]

Identifying Your Needs

Take a couple of minutes to fill out the following survey.

1. If a dollar bill reflected the way you and your spouse handle money, what might be the motto printed on it?

    ___ "In God we trust."

    ___ "Here today, gone tomorrow."

    ___ "You can't take that away from me."

    ___ "You're all I need."

    ___ "Caution: May cause violent behavior."

    ___ other _____

2. Which of the following do you feel most confident about? Least confident? Does your spouse "take up the slack" in areas where you feel least confident? If so, how?

    ___ deciding to make a big purchase

    ___ balancing a checkbook

    ___ finding bargains

    ___ making investments

    ___ earning money

    ___ paying bills

    ___ keeping track of a budget

    ___ other _____

3. Which of the following did you and your spouse discuss before you got married? Which did you not discuss but wish you had?

    ___ your financial goals

    ___ your debt

   ___ how you would use credit cards
   ___ whether both spouses would work
   ___ your family's attitude toward money
   ___ your beliefs about giving money to the church

4. How would you explain to a 10-year-old what "the value of a dollar" is? How does this compare to your spouse's answer?

_____

5. Name two necessities and two luxuries. How do your answers compare with those of your spouse? _____

_____

6. What's the best thing you've done with money since you got married? What made it such a positive experience? _____

_____

Watching and Discussing the DVD

No matter how the economy is doing, couples clash over cash—and credit, too. Family history, values, feelings about the future, self-discipline, self-esteem, and even math skills can contribute to the marital wealth wars.

    In this DVD segment, popular author and broadcaster Dave Ramsey talks about the money myths, mysteries, and mechanics that can spell the difference between lifelong bickering and financial peace. Host Dr. Greg Smalley adds a true tale from his own marriage, and urges viewers to work on the core issues that often underlie budget battles.

After viewing the DVD, use questions like these to help you think through what you saw and heard.

1. If you had a dollar for every time you and your spouse have disagreed about money, would you be rich? Why or why not?

2. Do you agree with the following Dave Ramsey quotes? Why or why not?
   - "Money is not the problem. What we are really fighting about here is who is in control."
   - "Budgeting together creates communication and cooperation over some of life's difficult subjects."
   - "Debt places huge relational pressures on marriages. . . . There is a sense of futility, this sense I am going to go really hard and get nowhere."

3. According to Dave, couples who fight about finances are really fighting about power, priorities, and passions. In which of those areas do you expect the most disagreement in the coming year? Why?

4. Which of the following do you think would create in a marriage what Dave calls a sense of infidelity or broken trust? How could that broken trust be restored?
   - having a checking account you haven't told your spouse about
   - forgetting to send in your car loan payment one month and keeping it a secret
   - running up $5,000 in credit card debt and not telling your spouse
   - promising your child a Disney World vacation without consulting your spouse

5. If you spent only what you'd budgeted in writing beforehand, how much would you have spent last week? Do you regret any purchases you made? Why or why not?

6. Is your marriage made up of a "nerd" and a "free spirit"? If so, how does that work when it comes to finances? If not, how would you describe the personality types of your spouse and yourself when it comes to money?

7. According to Dave, "The preacher didn't pronounce you a joint venture. He said, 'Now you are one.'" What's the difference? How could it affect the way spouses plan their saving, spending, and giving?

8. Do you have a "love drawer" in your home? If so, can you and your spouse name its contents? If not, can both of you name the locations of the documents that belong in that place?

Bible Study

> The plans of the diligent lead to profit as surely as haste leads to poverty.
> A fortune made by a lying tongue is a fleeting vapor and a deadly snare. . . .
> If a man shuts his ears to the cry of the poor, he too will cry out and not be answered. . . .
> He who loves pleasure will become poor; whoever loves wine and oil will never be rich. . . .

In the house of the wise are stores of choice food and oil, but a foolish man devours all he has.

He who pursues righteousness and love finds life, prosperity and honor. . . .

The sluggard's craving will be the death of him, because his hands refuse to work.

All day long he craves for more, but the righteous give without sparing. (Proverbs 21:5-6, 13, 17, 20-21, 25-26)

1. How would you and your spouse distill these proverbs into "Seven Rules for Financial Stability" that you both agree on?

   1.

   2.

   3.

   4.

   5.

   6.

   7.

A good name is more desirable than great riches; to be esteemed is better than silver or gold.

Rich and poor have this in common: The LORD is the Maker of them all.

A prudent man sees danger and takes refuge, but the simple keep going and suffer for it.

Humility and the fear of the LORD bring wealth and honor and life. . . .

The rich rule over the poor, and the borrower is servant to the lender. . . .

A generous man will himself be blessed, for he shares his food with the poor. . . .

He who oppresses the poor to increase his wealth and he who gives gifts to the rich—both come to poverty. . . .

Do not exploit the poor because they are poor and do not crush the needy in court, for the LORD will take up their case and will plunder those who plunder them. . . .

Do not be a man who strikes hands in pledge or puts up security for debts; if you lack the means to pay, your very bed will be snatched from under you. (Proverbs 22:1-4, 7, 9, 16, 22-23, 26, 27)

2. How would you and your spouse distill these proverbs into "Nine Financial Commandments" that you both agree on?

    1.
    2.
    3.
    4.
    5.
    6.
    7.
    8.
    9.

Keep your lives free from the love of money and be content with what you have, because God has said, "Never will I leave you; never will I forsake you." (Hebrews 13:5)

3. How does the second half of this verse explain the reason for the first half? If a husband and wife don't agree on the second half, can they agree on the first? If they do agree on the second half, will they necessarily obey the first? Why or why not?

Applying the Principles

Many couples clash over whether—and how—they need to change their financial habits. Here's an exercise to help you practice discussing that subject without causing bodily harm.

Look at the following ways to get better control of your finances. Your goal is to agree on the value of three of them, and to commit to doing one this week. Start by circling those you think make sense for most couples; your spouse should do the same.

1. Make separate lists for *necessary* expenses and those that are only *desirable*.
2. Look at grocery ads and plan your menu for the next month.
3. Avoid shopping without purpose, unless you're firmly committed not to buy while you're browsing.
4. Comparison-shop on the Internet; in brick-and-mortar stores, avoid buying anything that isn't on sale.
5. Plan errands so that gas isn't wasted by backtracking.
6. Buy a used car instead of a new one.
7. Borrow DVDs from the library instead of renting them; rent them instead of buying them.[12]
8. Have a weekly financial checkup.
9. Have a monthly budget planning meeting.
10. Make an annual inventory of your will, insurance, and location of key financial documents.

Draw a double circle around the suggestions that *both* of you chose. If you didn't both circle at least three, do your best to "sell" your spouse on the value of the ones you chose. Keep in mind that you're not committing to follow any of them yet.

When you've double-circled at least three suggestions, vote on which one you'll implement this week. If the vote is a tie, do a little "campaigning" for your choice and take another vote. If you still don't agree, talk it over and come up with a compromise that combines both of your choices or modifies one of them. For example, you might prefer to plan a week's worth of menus instead of a month's, or save money on DVDs by renting from a vending machine instead of a video store.

Encouragement from a Counselor

Some couples simply look around at their friends and neighbors, then base their outgo on what they think other people are spending. But in our materialistic culture, keeping up with the Joneses is a great way to get yourself in trouble financially. Instead, take a look at these five guidelines to consider when deciding how much to spend.

1. *Always spend less than you make.* This could be 80 percent of your take-home pay. Or, if you really want to be cautious, try 70 percent.

What happens to the remaining money? If you're spending 80 percent, put 10 percent into your tithe and 10 percent into savings and retirement. If you decide to spend 70 percent, put 10 percent into tithe, 10 percent into savings, and 10 percent into retirement.

Why not spend it all? Psalm 24:1 says, "The earth is the LORD's, and everything in it." When we recognize this, we understand that none of "our" money is really ours. God entrusts it to us to use as stewards. Being good guardians of those funds includes giving a portion back to God and using a portion to prepare for the future.

2. *Establish a budget.* This will help you consistently spend less than you make. Try basing it on a three-month average of your expenses.

To begin, find out exactly what you're spending and where. Many couples have found it works for each spouse to keep a notepad or extra checking account register handy so that each transaction can be written down. At the end of the week or month, compare your two records. Use the average of what you're spending in each area.

Don't be surprised if this is an eye-opening—even unsettling—experience. You may find that you're spending far more in a particular area than you thought.

3. *Set limits and stick to them.* Once you've established your budget, it's time to implement it.

Let's say you're overspending in one category by $50. That money has to come from somewhere. Look in your other categories and get the money from there.

The goal is to stay within your total budget. You may want to build in a "Miscellaneous" category or a cushion to cover overspending or unforeseen expenses.

4. *Be creative.* If an idea helps you stick with your budget, try it. You may want to set up a bill-paying method that fits your paydays, for instance. If you're paid twice a month, you might be able to satisfy part of a bill with the first paycheck and the rest with the second. A variation on this plan would be to pay bills in certain categories with the first paycheck and other categories with the second.

5. *Be open to change.* Review your spending monthly, or even weekly if necessary. Modify your budget as needed. After all, your account balance today will be different from what it was yesterday—and different from what it will be tomorrow. Knowing what and when to change takes constant monitoring.

In the case of Phil and Teri, change was a necessity. With the help of a counselor, they set up a plan.

First, they realized they had to forgive each other for all the pain they'd caused with their spending habits and poor communication about finances.

Second, they prayed together for a new beginning.

Third, they established a budget and a plan to get out of debt.

Taking these steps gave Phil and Teri more freedom to decide where their money would go, rather than being enslaved by bills. Being able to direct their funds instead of just finding them mysteriously gone at the end of the month helped the couple feel more capable of making informed spending decisions.

Phil and Teri gained a bright outlook on the future—and a revitalized sense of working together rather than being at odds with each other. As they found, time spent bickering over spending habits is time wasted. Marriage is more satisfying—and glorifying to God—if you're working as a team.

—Sandra Lundberg
Licensed Psychologist[13]

NOTES

1. Adapted from Sheryl DeWitt, "What Can I Do About My Spouse's Irritating Habits?" in *Complete Guide to the First Five Years of Marriage* (Carol Stream, Ill.: Focus on the Family/Tyndale House Publishers, 2006), p. 34.
2. Ibid, pp. 34-36.
3. Adapted from Rob Jackson, "What If We Don't Like the Same Things?" in *Complete Guide to the First Five Years of Marriage*, p. 161.
4. Ibid, pp. 161-163.
5. Adapted from Sandra Lundberg, "Are We Doing It Right?" in *Complete Guide to the First Five Years of Marriage*, p. 164.
6. Ibid, pp. 165-167.
7. Adapted from Romie Hurley, "What If an Argument Gets Out of Control?" in *Complete Guide to the First Five Years of Marriage*, p. 260.
8. Ibid, pp. 260-262.
9. Adapted from Phillip J. Swihart, "What If My Spouse Needs Psychological Help?" in *Complete Guide to the First Five Years of Marriage*, pp. 407-408.
10. Ibid, pp. 408-409.
11. Adapted from Sandra Lundberg, "How Much Should We Spend?" in *Complete Guide to the First Five Years of Marriage*, p. 114.
12. Items 1-7 adapted from Daniel Huerta, "How Can We Cut Our Expenses?" in *Complete Guide to the First Five Years of Marriage*, p. 134.
13. Adapted from Sandra Lundberg, "How Much Should We Spend?" in *Complete Guide to the First Five Years of Marriage*, pp. 114-116.

About Our DVD Presenters
Essentials of Marriage: Handle with Care

After suffering the loss of a $4 million real estate portfolio, **Dave Ramsey** decided to return to the basics of personal finance and help others. Dave is the author of the New York Times best-selling books *Financial Peace* and *The Total Money Makeover*. He is also the host of the nationally syndicated *Dave Ramsey Show*. Many national corporations as well as tens of thousands of individuals have benefited from his Financial Peace University program and his live seminars. He and his wife, Sharon, live in Nashville and have three children.

Dr. John Trent is president of the Center for Strong Families and StrongFamilies.com, an organization that trains leaders to launch and lead marriage and family programs in their churches and communities. John speaks at conferences across the country and has written or cowritten more than a dozen award-winning and bestselling books, including *The 2 Degree Difference* and the million-selling parenting classic *The Blessing* with Gary Smalley. His books, of which there are more than two million in print, have been translated into 11 languages. John has been a featured guest on radio and television programs including *Focus on the Family*, *The 700 Club*, and CNN's *Sonya Live in L.A.* John and his wife, Cindy, have been married for 28 years and have two daughters.

Dr. Archibald Hart is well known for his ministry to churches through psychological training, education, and consultation. A former dean of the School of Psychology at Fuller Theological Seminary, he is now retired from full-time teaching but continues to examine issues of stress, depression, and anxiety. Dr. Hart is the author of 24 books, including *Thrilled to Death*, *Stressed or Depressed*, and *Safe Haven Marriage*. Dr. Hart and his wife, Kathleen, live in California. They have three daughters and seven grandchildren.

Since founding Precept Ministries International with her husband, Jack, in 1970 with the vision to establish people in God's Word, international Bible teacher and four-time Gold Medallion award-winning author **Kay Arthur** has written more than 100 books and Bible studies. Kay is also the teacher and host of *Precepts for Life*, a radio and television program that reaches a worldwide viewing audience of over 94 million, teaching them how to discover truth for themselves. Today, God is using Precept Ministries to reach nearly 150 countries with inductive Bible studies translated into nearly 70 languages. Kay serves as executive vice president and shares the office of Precept CEO with Jack. The Arthurs live in Chattanooga, Tennessee.

Dr. Gary and Barb Rosberg, cofounders of America's Family Coaches, host a nationally syndicated daily radio program and have conducted conferences on marriage and family relationships in more than 100 cities across the country. The Rosbergs have written more than a dozen prominent marriage and family resources, including *The 5 Love Needs of Men & Women* (a Gold Medallion finalist) and *Divorce-Proof Your Marriage* (a Gold Medallion winner). Gary earned his Ed.D. from Drake University and has been a marriage and family counselor for more than 25 years. Married more than 30 years, the Rosbergs live outside Des Moines, Iowa, and have two married daughters and four grandchildren.

Dr. Greg Smalley earned his doctorate in clinical psychology from Rosemead School of Psychology at Biola University. He also holds master's degrees in counseling psychology (Denver Seminary) and clinical psychology (Rosemead School of Psychology). Greg is president of Smalley Marriage Institute, a marriage and family ministry in Branson, Missouri, and serves as chairman of the board of the National Marriage Association. Greg has published more than 100 articles on parenting and relationship issues. He is the coauthor of *The DNA of Parent-Teen Relationships* (with his father, Gary Smalley) and *The Men's Relational Toolbox* (with his father and his brother, Michael). Greg, his wife, Erin, and their three children live in Branson, Missouri.

Gary Thomas is a writer and the founder/director of the Center for Evangelical Spirituality, a speaking and writing ministry that combines Scripture, history, and the Christian classics. His books include *Sacred Marriage*, *Authentic Faith* (winner of the Gold Medallion award in 2003), and *Seeking the Face of God*. Gary has spoken in 49 states and four countries and has served as the campus pastor at Western Seminary, where he is an adjunct professor. Gary, his wife, Lisa, and their three kids live in Bellingham, Washington.

Dr. Julianna Slattery is a family psychologist for Focus on the Family. Juli is the author of *Finding the Hero in Your Husband*, *Guilt-Free Motherhood*, and *Beyond the Masquerade*. Applying biblical wisdom to the everyday lives of women and families is her passion. She shares her message with a combination of humor, candor, and foundational truth. Juli earned a doctor of psychology and master of science in clinical psychology at Florida Institute of Technology, a master of arts in psychology from Biola University, and a bachelor of arts from Wheaton College. Juli and her husband, Mike, live in Colorado Springs and are the parents of three boys.

Mitch Temple is a licensed marriage and family therapist and author of *The Marriage Turnaround*. He holds two graduate degrees, in ministry and in marriage and family therapy, from Southern Christian University. Mitch currently serves as the director of the marriage department at Focus on the Family in Colorado Springs. He has conducted intensives nationwide for couples on the brink of divorce and has served as a family, pulpit, and counseling minister in churches for a total of 23 years. He was director of pastoral care, small groups, family ministry, and a counseling center at a large church for 13 years. He and his wife, Rhonda, have been married for more than 24 years and have three children.

FOCUS ON THE FAMILY®

Welcome to the Family

Whether you purchased this book, borrowed it, or received it as a gift, we're glad you're reading it. It's just one of the many helpful, encouraging, and biblically based resources produced by Focus on the Family® for people in all stages of life.

Focus began in 1977 with the vision of one man, Dr. James Dobson, a licensed psychologist and author of numerous best-selling books on marriage, parenting, and family. Alarmed by the societal, political, and economic pressures that were threatening the existence of the American family, Dr. Dobson founded Focus on the Family with one employee and a once-a-week radio broadcast aired on 36 stations.

Now an international organization reaching millions of people daily, Focus on the Family is dedicated to preserving values and strengthening and encouraging families through the life-changing message of Jesus Christ.

Focus on the Family MAGAZINES

These faith-building, character-developing publications address the interests, issues, concerns, and challenges faced by every member of your family from preschool through the senior years.

For More INFORMATION

 ONLINE:
Log on to
FocusOnTheFamily.com
In Canada, log on to
FocusOnTheFamily.ca

 PHONE:
Call toll-free:
800-A-FAMILY
(232-6459)
In Canada, call toll-free:
800-661-9800

FOCUS ON THE FAMILY® MAGAZINE	FOCUS ON THE FAMILY CLUBHOUSE JR.® Ages 4 to 8	FOCUS ON THE FAMILY CLUBHOUSE® Ages 8 to 12	FOCUS ON THE FAMILY CITIZEN® U.S. news issues

Rev. 12/08

More Great Resources
from Focus on the Family®

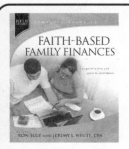

Complete Guide to Faith-Based Family Finances
By Ron Blue and Jeremy White
Whether you're a financial whiz, a financial novice, or somewhere in between, the *Complete Guide to Faith-Based Family Finances* is filled with commonsense, practical tools to help you make wise financial decisions year after year. In addition to covering every area of financial planning, this helpful resource contains the answers to many of the questions asked by families like yours. Hardcover.

The Way to Love Your Wife: Creating Greater Love and Passion in the Bedroom
By Clifford L. Penner, Ph.D. and Joyce J. Penner, M.N., R.N.
The Way to Love Your Wife is a book on marital sex directed to men with the purpose of changing their attitude and approach toward sex. It helps take the pressure off of both spouses to perform or achieve certain results and gives the man the confidence he needs to know and understand how to meet his wife's needs. By doing so, both husband and wife will find sex more fulfilling. Paperback.

Healing the Hurt in Your Marriage: Beyond Discouragement, Anger, and Resentment to Forgiveness
By Dr. Gary and Barbara Rosberg
Learn how to close the loop on unresolved conflict by practicing forgiving love. Marriage experts Dr. Gary and Barbara Rosberg draw from biblical wisdom to offer a step-by-step process that will move you beyond conflict to restore hope, harmony, and intimacy in your marriage today. Paperback.

FOR MORE INFORMATION

Online:
Log on to FocusOnTheFamily.com
In Canada, log on to focusonthefamily.ca.

Phone:
Call toll free: 800-A-FAMILY
In Canada, call toll free: 800-661-9800.

BPZZXP1